Finding the Center of the World

Midwestern Environmental Spirituality

Peter Bakken
Nancy Adams-Cogan
Rod Strampe

Harvest Books
Ice Cube Press
North Liberty, Iowa

Finding the Center of The World:
Midwestern Environmental Spirituality.

©2003 Peter Bakken, Nancy Adams-Cogan & Rod Strampe
©2004 second printing, slighty revised first edition

Ice Cube Press
205 N Front St
North Liberty, Iowa 52317-9302
p 319/626-2055
f 413/451-0223
icecube@inav.net
www.icecubepress.com

ISBN #1-888160-05-5

Library of Congress Control Number: 2003110991

No portion of this book may be reproduced in any way without permission of the authors except for brief quotations for review, or educational work. In which case the publisher and author(s) shall be provided copies.

Manufactured in the United States of America

The paper used in this publication meets the minimum requirements of the ⊛American National Standard for Information Sciences—Permanence of Paper for Printed Library Materials, ANSI Z39.48-1992

This book is a companion publication of the Sixth Harvest Lecture. An annual event planned and organized through the Standing By Words Center, a(501)c(3), a non-profit, educational organization accepting tax-deductible contributions, donations and volunteer help in order to provide public events on the Midwest. FMI e-mail: WordsCtr@yahoo.com, or check out http://www.jccniowa.org/~WordsCtr

†
'The Discovery or projection of a fixed point
—the center—
is equivalent to the creation of the world…'

Mircea Eliade
The Sacred & The Profane
†

We always
start by giving thanks—

begin slowly
searching the air for gold
panning the universe for treasure
finding 'centers'
in unthinkable places,
accidently
in the nest of a
Great Blue Heron
beneath the
shadow of
a barn...
long live the harvest!

Special thanks for this year's publication
& Harvest Lecture go to:

▲Humanities Iowa
▲Daniel and Ann Krumm Foundation
▲Philip Knutson Family Endowment
▲Iowa Arts Council
▲Lutheran Campus Ministry ELCA, Univ. of Iowa
▲Southeast Iowa Synod ELCA, Environmental Task Force
▲Board Members of the Standing By Words Center
▲Dennis Reese at WSUI Radio
▲Good & steadfast words from Thomas Dean
▲University of Iowa Student Government

†

CONTENTS

THE GRACE OF PLACE
Patriotism & the Care of the Earth.
Peter Bakken

ROADSCAPES: CENTRAL USA
Poetry by Nancy Adams-Cogan

MIDWESTERN ROADSCAPES
Photography by Rod Strampe

†

THE GRACE OF PLACE:
Patriotism and the Care of the Earth.

Introduction: The Sense of Place

When I was in graduate school in the early 1980's, I worked for a few years as a church secretary in the neighborhood of the University of Chicago. One day, I received a call from a company offering me a great deal on office supplies. I had learned to be wary of such calls; one common scam was to call a church to "verify" a "standing order" for office supplies before shipping—a standing order that had, in fact, never been placed, but which a new or absent-minded office worker might trustingly assume *had* been, and wind up with a box full of electric typewriter ribbons that had exceeded their shelf life. I was, therefore, leery of ordering anything from a company known to me only by a phone call. So I asked to be sent a catalog or printed material. That, I was told, was not available. Well, then, what was the company's address? We don't do business by mail, I was told. Irritated and more than merely suspicious by this point, I asked, Where was the company located? Again, I could not get a straight answer. Finally, exasperated by the telemarketer's evasiveness, I demanded, (to the surprise and amusement of the pastor in the adjoining office) *"Where are YOU sitting RIGHT AT THIS MOMENT?"*

I don't remember if he gave me an answer, hung up, or what. It hardly mattered; the scam was transparent, and the conversation had been reduced to absurdity. But at least I had the meager satisfaction of backing him up against the wall of an undeniable, if seemingly empty, truth: everybody has to be someplace.

But is this only an empty truth, a mere tautology or truism? Or is the undeniable and universal fact that we each always find ourselves in a particular place in the world something worth pondering? Might it possibly even have *theological* significance?

A half century ago, a professor at the Chicago Lutheran Seminary in Maywood, Illinois, named Joseph Sittler wrote one of his occasional columns, "The Grace Note," for the seminary's quarterly newsletter. In it, he stated that:

> Man not only loves the earth; he has added grace whereby he is attached to and lovingly related to his own corner of God's creation with a peculiar pathos and affection. Patriotism, so understood, is a disposition that grows out of a man's organic relation to his own land as plain lovable geography!—as a complex of trees and rivers and streets, of stacks and railroad yards and municipal dumps and the monstrous repeated pattern of the city.[1]

Sittler was an important pioneer in the development of an ecological theology, as one of the first 20th Century theologians to publically engage environmental issues as a critical religious problem. This essay is of interest as perhaps the first published indication of what would become one of his major themes: a theology of the natural world as

---

1. [Joseph Sittler], "The Grace Note," *The Chicago Lutheran Seminary Record* 56, no. 2 (April 1951): 2-3. The essay is unsigned, but is unmistakably Sittler's. I have chosen not to edit this and later quotations by Sittler for inclusive language, not because I believe that eliminating sexism from our language is unimportant, but for the following reasons: (1) Given the number of synonyms for, say, "man," there is the difficulty in choosing the right word. It is especially daunting when reworking the words of a writer so attuned to nuances of language and so distinctive, almost idiosyncratic, in his style of expression, as Sittler. (2) Bracketed substitutions or "[*sic*]" would draw attention toward the changed or flagged word in itself and away from the point of the whole passage. (3) To simply revise the passage would come close to falsifying history in order make Sittler seem more enlightened—in terms of our current standards for inclusive language—than he was.

a "theater of grace." But this essay also strikingly anticipates current concerns about threats to "place" and attachment to place.

Anxiety about the fate of place in contemporary human experience has a number of facets. One concern is the continuing influence of the general attitude of detachment from and disinterest in the material world that is the legacy of some strands in the spirituality of Western Christendom. Another is the predisposition of much post-Enlightenment thought toward universal, general, and abstract principles of rationality over against the particular, local, and concrete stuff of everyday life and feeling. More recent developments in the affluent and industrialized world also have a corrosive effect on the character and uniqueness of particular places, and on people's "sense of place:" One, of which Sittler was acutely aware around the time of this essay, is the increasing mobility that has characterized post-World War II America.

> Our American lives are impoverished if they lack a sense of identity with the country around them and are ignorant of its written and anecdotal history. The rootlessness of American life has here a part of its cause, we sit lightly to places and people; we are in large part a migrant population. Frontier psychology has persisted beyond the disappearance of the frontier. We belong to a lot of things; not many of us retain a sense of belonging to a place or pattern of life. No wonder then that a corporation chartered in Delaware, doing business in Ohio, directed from New York, can airily transfer members of its staff from New Jersey to Illinois without batting an eye over the human dislocations involved.[2]

Place and sense of place are also increasingly under attack from radical, destructive changes in the places themselves: environmental devastation and degradation from abuse, pollution, and insensitive and unintelligent forms of "development" that impose the bland homogeneity of cookie-cutter suburban development, fast-food chains and "big box" superstores, acres of parking, and multilane expressways. Mass communication media and the Internet create a virtual reality accessible anywhere, anytime, that seems more real to people than the

---

2. Sittler, "Grace Note," 3.

land on which they live. Extreme individualism disengages people from neighborhood and community. And so on.[3]

In the pages that follow, I will refer frequently to this and other writings by Sittler as I develop the claim that, for the sake of both the care of the earth and our spiritual health, "place"—not just "nature" or "the environment" or "creation," but particular, concrete, identifiable *places*—and "grace" must be brought together and understood in the light of each other. Being "placed" is an essential aspect of our being creatures and recipients of God's grace. Conscious, intentional deepening and working out of our sense of placement is integral to living out our human vocation. That vocation, at least in part, takes the form of seeking to safeguard the integrity of places—our own, and those we affect at a distance. I will suggest three different but complementary metaphors for understanding the meaning of place: container, constellation, and lens. Each of these metaphors highlights different ways that being in a place and being attached to that place can be forms of grace, and together they illuminate the true meaning of "patriotism."

---

3. The literature of "sense of place" is voluminous, and I will not begin to encapsulate it here. However, the following titles, which have informed my own thinking, will indicate the modest but growing theological literature on the topic: Linda M. Graber, *Wilderness as Sacred Space* (Washington, D.C.: Association of American Geographers, 1976); Walter Brueggemann, *The Land: Place as Gift, Promise and Challenge in Biblical Faith* (Minneapolis: Fortress Press, 1977; 2nd ed. 2002); Belden C. Lane, *Landscapes of the Sacred: Geography and Narrative in American Spirituality* (Mahwah, N.J.: Paulist Press, 1988); Geoffrey R. Lilburne, *A Sense of Place: A Christian Theology of the Land* (Nashville: Abingdon Press, 1989); George E. Tinker, "The Full Circle of Liberation: An American Indian Theology of Place," *Sojourners* 21 (October 1992), 12-17; "A Sense of Place" in *All Creation Is Groaning: An Interdisciplinary Vision for Life in a Sacred Universe*, ed. Carol J. Dempsey and Russell A. Butkus (Collegeville, Minn: Liturgical Press, 1999), 240-268; William P. Brown, *The Ethos of the Cosmos: The Genesis of Moral Imagination in the Bible* (Grand Rapids, Mich.: Eerdmans, 1999); T. J. Gorringe, *Theology of the Built Environment: Justice, Empowerment, Redemption* (Cambridge: Cambridge University Press, 2002).

An Autobiogeographical Excursion

In drawing on the writings of Sittler, and also on those of the Aldo Leopold, the pioneering conservationist and ecologist from the first half of the 20th Century, I am reflecting something of my own sense of place. Except for occasional excursions farther afield, I have lived within a narrow ellipse that reaches from the eastern edge of North Dakota to the northeastern corner of Illinois, some 600 or 700 miles long. I have realized only lately that, at least according to some maps, my life has been largely within what was in presettlement times the realm of the eastern tallgrass prairie or the transition zone between it and the Great Lakes Forest, and on land shaped by the Wisconsin stage of glaciation in the late Pleistocene Epoch over 10,000 years ago.

I was born and raised in Fargo, North Dakota. The town lies on the eastern border of North Dakota, along the Red River of the North, which flows north to Hudson Bay through an agriculturally rich and very flat prairie land that was once the bottom of Glacial Lake Agassiz. My parents grew up in the northeastern corner of the state—my father on a farm, and my mother in a small town. I attended Concordia College, just across the river in Moorhead, Minnesota.

The other end of my ellipse was fixed when I went to the University of Chicago Divinity School for graduate study in theology. (*National Geographic* once described Chicago as "a city bounded on one side by infinity," referring to Lake Michigan. That sounded like an ideal place to study theology.) Sittler had taught at the Divinity School until his retirement in 1974 and though aging and nearly blind, he was still a vital presence around the University and nearby Lutheran seminary, speaking, preaching and mentoring students. (He had served as interim pastor at the church where I later worked as secretary, and was a member there.) In the course of casting about for a dissertation topic I hit upon the still relatively unexplored topic of "theology of ecology." Sittler's pioneering theology—still fresh and stimulating in spite of all the later developments in that field—became one of my guiding stars.

Another was Aldo Leopold, whose importance in my developing understanding grew as I followed my wife, a student at the Lutheran School of Theology at Chicago, to Wisconsin. Her year-long internship was in Baraboo, Wisconsin, nestled in a canoe-shaped outcropping of purplish Precambrian quartzite at the edge of the Driftless area—that area in Wisconsin, Minnesota, Iowa, and Illinois left uncovered by the most recent Ice Age glaciers. Though born and raised in Iowa, educated at Yale, and having worked with the Forestry Service in the Southwest, Leopold came to teach game management, and later wildlife ecology, at the University of Wisconsin-Madison. While there, he purchased property along the Wisconsin River just north of Baraboo, forty miles from Madison, where he and his family spent vacations and weekends restoring the abused and abandoned land and refurbishing the old chicken coop that became famous as "The Shack." This was the setting for the essays that formed the first section of *A Sand County Almanac*, often called "the Bible of the environmental movement."

After returning to Chicago for my wife's senior year, we came back to Wisconsin for her first call to a parish in Black Earth (so named for the rich black prairie soils of the area), and later calls to rural Stoughton and Madison. I have worked for most of this time for the Au Sable Institute of Environmental Studies, in an office in Madison near the University (although most of the Institute's programs are conducted at its campuses in Michigan and Washington.) Though I needed a car to commute while we lived outside of Madison, I am now able to bike to work regularly over half the year, which has enriched my "sense of place" enormously.

Sittler and Leopold not only have associations for me with places I have lived. Their attentiveness to the lived experience of the landscape in all its subtlety and complexity, its human and natural and spiritual dimensions, has been a powerful incentive to deepen my own awareness and appreciation for the places I live in or visit. Although I can't claim a very high level of achievement in this regard, what capacities for a sense of place that I have been able to cultivate have informed and are the experiential background of the exploration that follows.

Place as Container

We commonly think of "place" as a bounded space or region. It is "turf," "territory," "home ground;" we are apt to think of a house on its lot, a park, a city, a state or a country. The implied image is that of a container. A container separates what is "inside" from what is "outside," but at the same time holds together whatever is "inside" it. So understood, a place is inclusive: Its contents comprise whatever happen to be found within its boundaries—human beings with their institutions, societies and cultures; land forms, waters, plants, animals, buildings, fields, gardens, streets, tools and works of art, and so on. "Place" therefore cuts across our abstract categories of nature and culture, human and nonhuman, aesthetic and utilitarian, etc. It embraces all these in a way that they have to be considered *together*.

At the same time, a place is exclusive: it is set off from the larger space of its environment and from other spaces, delimited by a boundary separating *here* from *there*, *this* place from *that* place. A shelter is a place that makes life possible by creating a space of relative security and comfort over against "the outside world"— e.g., the "little house on the prairie" that, though humble and primitive, keeps out the wind, the cold, the rain, the snow, the wolf and the enemy.

The "container" conception of place highlights our existence as finite, earthbound beings. The biblical understanding of creatureliness, as Sittler pointed out, involves "limits and boundaries to our living":

> There is a limit which stands not only at the end of human life as death, but which is built into the structure of human life by virtue of its creaturely character. All birth and development, all unfolding and enterprise, all moral vision and achievement are not only enfolded within this limit but receive their urgent character from it. Here is a 'given' time, a 'given' space, a 'given' possibility. Within the boundaries of this 'given' there are, to be sure, vast and absolutely crucial possibilities for affirmation or denial, hearing or deafness, decision or stasis—but no elaboration of these possibilities can avoid the limit of sin and death.[4]

Such an understanding of creatureliness as finitude includes the particularities of place, as bounded space, as an essential ingredient, as well as "the limit of sin and death." Where we are limits us; it may put a crimp on our freedom of movement, but it also contributes to making us who we are.

Our creatureliness includes our corporeality as "earthly" beings, beings whose place is "earth." We are not just "embodied" beings, but we are also "embedded" within the biophysical, material world, which we can experience with all our senses. As I have found, how one gets around within a place can make a difference in how one experiences that place. Commuting by bike, I can feel the postglacial character of the terrain as I struggle up one drumlin or end moraine after another, just as I can feel the sun and wind and catch the scent of lilac blossoms or notice landscaping or architectural details of the homes I pass by—experiences denied to me when rushing past in a car or bus, well-sealed within. And, as earthly creatures we are vulnerable to what is "out there" in our environment—West Nile virus, tornadoes (like the one that took the roof off my family's house in Fargo when I was still *in utero*), freezing cold, deadly heat waves, and ultraviolet light.

How does this aspect of our experience of place relate to the theological concept of grace? By Sittler's definition, "The fundamental meaning of grace is the goodness and loving-kindness of God and the activity of this goodness in and toward his creation."[5] Grace, for Sittler, meant more than just the forgiveness of sins that is offered by God in Christ; while that remained for him the central, focal meaning of grace, its full scope was much larger.

The "container" metaphor brings into focus grace as the gift of habitat. Genesis 1 depicts the gracious action of God in creating different places for different forms of life to dwell. Creation takes place through acts of separation—light from darkness; the waters above the dome of the sky from those below it; the dry land from the seas. The seven days and their respective works first mark off the different domains of creation—day and night (day one), sky and water (day two), and land with its vegetation (day three). Then those places are filled with the creatures who are to inhabit them: sun, moon and stars (day four), birds and water creatures (day five), and finally land animals—including human beings (day six).

The theme of the gift of place continues through the rest of the Bible. In Genesis 2, Adam is "placed" in the garden of Eden (which is described with notable geographic detail). The Hebrew Scriptures go on to tell

---

4. Joseph Sittler, *The Ecology of Faith: The New Situation in Preaching* (Philadelphia: Fortress Press, 1961), 23.

5. Joseph Sittler, "Excerpts from *Essays on Nature and Grace*" in Steven Bouma-Prediger and Peter Bakken, eds., *Evocations of Grace: Writings on Ecology, Theology and Ethics* (Grand Rapids, Mich.: Eerdmans, 2000), 92.

the story of the gift of the Promised Land to the people of Israel, their exile from the land, and their promised return to it. In the Incarnation, "the Word became flesh and dwelt [literally, 'pitched a tent'] among us" (John 1:14) in a particular time and place. Even the vision of the "last things" in the Christian Scriptures looks forward to a new heaven and a new earth, described in terms of a human habitation (a city, the New Jerusalem), within which there is also a place for nature—the river of the water of life and the tree of life (Rev. 21-22). Thus, the primal gift of divine grace, the gift of being, is the gift of a particular place to be.

If, as Sittler suggests, attachment to place is a form of grace, identification with a place—as an ingredient in one's sense of one's own identity, and as loyalty to and protectiveness of one's place almost as an extension of oneself—may be one aspect of that form of grace. The place that is our home, or our origin (or, for some people, the series of places) is constitutive of our identity, though it certainly does not exhaust it. The linkage between place and identity is evident in the conventional question we often use in conversation with a new acquaintance: "where are you from, originally?"—reflecting the assumption that to know where someone is from adds some detail, texture, depth and solidity to our sense of who they are.

Sittler speaks of attachment in terms of "loving identification with one's own land," which suggests a feeling that what happens to one's own land, or place, happens to oneself. If it is insulted, I am offended; if it is degraded, I am grieved and perhaps personally diminished; if it is attacked, I am threatened; if it is honored or prosperous or successful, I feel buoyed up with a personal sense of pride. We see this in hometown fans' attachment to their home team. But it is especially a part of the "patriotism," as we have seen in the wake of the September 11 attacks, to the extent that those events awakened a sense of common identity as Americans and bonds of sympathy with our fellow Americans in New York, Washington DC, and the families and friends of those aboard the planes. There is a sense of solidarity with others that arises simply from the fact that one shares a common place.

However, the exclusion implied by the place as container metaphor all to often has tragic consequences. Boundaries also distinguish the "insider" from the "outsider." Throughout history, having a place often has meant the dis-placing of others—as when, bolstered by lofty claims to divine entitlement and "manifest destiny," our own nation expanded at the expense of the original inhabitants of the land.

Not far from where we lived in Black Earth, on the bluffs along the Wisconsin River, is the site of the Battle of Wisconsin Heights. There, in 1832, a Sac war chief named Black Hawk and 60 warriors held off more than 700 U.S. soldiers, allowing hundreds of women, children and elders to escape across the Wisconsin River. They had crossed from Iowa to Illinois to try to reclaim their tribal lands, and had eluded their pursuers through Illinois and Wisconsin (along the way passing through what is now Madison). The victory was short lived, for the tribe was finally caught and massacred before they could cross back over the Mississippi. (In 1990, the Wisconsin Legislature formally apologized to the Sac and Fox Nations. The apology was accepted.)

Even in the absence of such overt conflict, to know one's place is to define it over against, perhaps even in antithesis to, the "other" places. The sense of identification with one's own land can foster attitudes of smug superiority to, suspicion of, or outright hostility to "foreigners" and "foreign" lands. And so the "container" becomes a fortress, and security is defined as making boundaries impermeable to external threats: airport security, border patrols, and walls crowned with razor wire, all backed up by military force.

Thus, the metaphor of place as "container" focuses our attention on the gift of a particular place as a habitat within which both humankind and otherkind can flourish, but it can also reinforce a dangerous narrowing of our vision and sympathy. How do these destructive possibilities of attachment to place square with Sittler's assertion that "Loving, personal identification with one's own land has never been a breeder of arrogant nationalism"?[6]—for that is as good a label as any for what seems to be one potential negative by-product of attachment to place. Is there another metaphor that might help us grasp the unity and integrity of particular places without placing so much emphasis on boundaries, borders, and limits?

PLACE AS CONSTELLATION

The second metaphor I would like to propose is that of "place as constellation"—that is, an association of interconnected things within a region of space. To some extent, this image has been implicit in the preceding discussion of the container metaphor, inasmuch as a container implies contents. This metaphor, however, shifts the emphasis from the container to the things it contains and the relationships among them, which are what give a place its identity, integrity, and individuality.

Take, for example, the states that make up the USA. On a map, we may recognize states by their distinctive shapes, but the shape of their boundary tells us nothing about them as places, except perhaps indirectly (e.g., an irregular border usually means a river or a coastline). By contrast, what gives a state its identity and character is the culture of its inhabitants, the contours of its terrain, its prevalent forms of industry and land use, the size and distribution of its urban centers, its native fauna and flora, outstanding structural landmarks and natural features, etc. These cannot be understood without tracing the ways in which geological, ecological, political, cultural, and economic processes and products have interacted with one another in that part of the country.

From this angle, one's relationship to a place is a matter of one's place in the web of relationships between the beings it contains or includes. Think, for example, of all that is bundled together in the experience of settling into a place: If one lives or stays for some time in a place, one develops a sense of that place as having an shape and an internal structure that is defined by one's activities, interests, and relationships to the persons and things that it contains. It is one's "home range" or turf, defined by the routes of regular routines and occasional side-trips, out of which gradually develops a sense of orientation, a "mental map" by which one knows where one is relative to particular objects and buildings and where they are relative to one another, how to get from one to the other. In time, there emerges a degree of comfort, a sense of relative security and of being "settled in" if not "at home;" it becomes

---

6. Sittler, "Grace Note," 3.

possible to relax and move easily in an environment that is an ordered cosmos rather than a chaos.

Also with the passage of time, the place becomes the matrix of a developing network of relationships to others; it is the medium in which are embedded one's connections to the persons, objects, animals, trees and buildings for whom one feels an affinity, affection, or kinship as neighbors or parts of the neighborhood.

One memorable episode in our own "settling in" to our neighborhood occurred one spring evening when my wife, daughter and I were walking by the small park down the street from our new house. We curiously approached a group of neighbors—whom we had not yet met—whose attention seemed focused on the marshy pond on the other side of a screen of trees. Asking what was up, we were told that a pair of sandhill cranes had been heard somewhere by the edge of the pond. We proceeded to listen for the cranes ourselves and to have an enjoyable time getting to know our new neighbors—the ice broken by a bird that Leopold once called "the trumpet in the orchestra of evolution…the symbol of our untamable past, of that incredible sweep of millennia which underlies and conditions the daily affairs of birds and men,"[7]

Memories, stories heard from others, and knowledge of the natural and human history of a place add a temporal dimension to the way in which one experiences the reality and particularity of that place. (Leopold: "A sense of time lies thick and heavy [on the crane marsh].… Our appreciation of the crane grows with the slow unraveling of earthly history. His tribe, we now know, stems out of the remote Eocene."[8]) That place can also be a field for activity—homemaking, gardening and landscaping, participation in community projects or in the civic and political life of the community, and so on—activities by which one (hopefully) enhances the private or public sectors in that place, and which create new relationships and add new dimensions to one's understanding of what happens in that place, and what makes

---

7. Aldo Leopold, *A Sand County Almanac with Sketches Here and There* (New York: Oxford University Press, 1949), 96.
8. Ibid.

it the kind of place it is. In a miniscule way, our family's experience of beginning to turn part of our back yard into a prairie wildflower garden—with plants obtained from a neighbor on the next street—is one episode in the history of the changes in this landscape. What would the farmer who busted the prairie have thought if he or she had imagined that, decades after the farm had been turned into a suburb, its inhabitants would be trying (in however small a way) to *replant* the prairie?

To put this into a theological frame in terms of creation, we may say that our "creaturehood" is *co*-creaturehood, life not only on earth, in the material world, but life in interdependence with other material, earthly beings. Co-creaturehood means that to be is to be with, among other beings—most immediately, the beings that make up or share one's place. As Canadian theologian Douglas John Hall argues, "Being means being-with."[9] There is no creature that is an isolated individual, separate and independent from all other beings.

The corresponding dimension of grace is the gift of life in and through the community of creation. The portrait of creation found in Psalm 104 expresses this gift of life-in-interdependence. As in Genesis, God is described in Psalm 104 as creating habitats for life. God establishes boundaries that make a space for life by keeping at bay "the waters," which in the world view of the ancient Near East represented unformed, primordial chaos—something not necessarily evil in itself, but a threat to life if it is not in its proper place (Ps. 104:5-9). Psalm 104 goes on to show how the diverse parts of creation form an integrated, interdependent whole. God's works are "manifold" (Ps. 104:24). The different species of creatures are associated with their particular habitats, but on a smaller, more intimate scale than in Genesis: "the high mountains are for the wild goats, the rocks are a refuge for the coneys" (Ps. 104:18, NRSV). The Psalm portrays creation ecologically: the storks live among the branches of the cedars that grow along the streams (Ps. 104:16-17).

---

9. Douglas John Hall, *Imaging God: Dominion as Stewardship* (Grand Rapids: Eerdmans, 1986), 113ff.

Sittler's exegesis of Psalm 104 affirms this web of interdependence as a manifestation of God's grace:

> In this Psalm nothing in the world of man and nothing in the world of nature is either independent or capable of solitary significance. Every upward arching phenomenon, every smallest thing, is derived from the fountain of life…The trees and the birds, the grass and the cattle, the plump vine and wine that gladdens the heart of man are all bound together in a bundle of grace…Natural and mortal life are incandescent with meaning because of their mutual dependence upon the will of the ultimate and Holy one…Here is a holy naturalism, a matrix of grace in which all things derive significance from their origin, and all things find fulfillment in praise.[10]

This understanding of grace in the ecological and communal structure of relationships within a place points to a different grounding for security than the maintenance of impermeable boundaries: security is a matter of healthy, supportive relationships with the land and with one's neighbors.

What, then, might the "place as constellation" metaphor tell us about the way our attachment to places might be a form of "common grace"? As the "place" that one is attached to is seen to be more concrete and richly textured than when viewed through the "container" metaphor alone, so is the sense of attachment more complex. It is more than a matter of identifying oneself with a place name or a label on a map—calling oneself an "American" or "North Dakotan" or "Chicagoan" simply on the basis of spatial location or origin. "Loving identification" is a matter of affection for, memory of, and personal acquaintance with particular landscapes, features, and inhabitants of that place.

Such attachment is a gift of greater openness to what that place has to offer. As Kathleen Dean Moore has written, to love a place means

> To want to be near it, physically…To want to know everything about it—its story, its moods, what it looks like by moonlight…To rejoice in the fact of it…To be transformed in its presence—lifted, lighter on your feet, transparent, open to everything beautiful and new…To want to be joined with it, taken in by it, lost in it.[11]

---

10. Sittler, "A Theology for Earth," in *Evocations of Grace*, 28.
11. Kathleen Dean Moore, "What Does it Mean to Love a Place?" *Aldo Leopold Foundation Newsletter*, Fall 2002, p. 2.

Love opens to knowledge, and knowledge of a place and its constituents frequently leads to greater delight in and deeper affection for them. Even a rudimentary knowledge of, say, architecture or botany gives meaning to seemingly insignificant details; it brings into focus what was formerly a vague and indistinct gray or green blur. To gain the sense of belonging that comes with being more fully oriented in and alive to a place; to develop the ability to call up before the mind's eye its history and prehistory, its hidden lives and subterranean secrets, is a positive enlargement of one's being. As Leopold told his students, "Once you learn to read the land, I have no fear of what you will do to it, or with it. And I know many pleasant things it will do to you."[12]

But such intimate knowledge of a place also brings an awareness of all that threatens, subverts, or is out of joint about it. Leopold also said,

> One of the penalties of an ecological education is that one lives alone in a world of wounds. Much of the damage inflicted on land is quite invisible to laymen. An ecologist must either harden his shell and make believe that the consequences of science are none of his business, or he must be the doctor who sees the marks of death in a community that believes itself well and does not want to be told otherwise.[13]

Grief and loss are an inescapable part of attachment to places. This is especially true in an age of accelerating environmental degradation and urban sprawl. The elegiac tone of many of the essays in *Sand County Almanac* give eloquent witness to that as Leopold mourns the passing of the passenger pigeon, the tallgrass prairie, the deltas of the Rio Grande, and anticipates (prematurely) the extinction of the sandhill crane. Such awareness can be a powerful motive to work to protect and restore the character and integrity of the place. Moore also lists these aspects of what it means to love a place: "To fear its loss, and grieve for its injuries…To protect it—fiercely, mindlessly, futilely, and

---

12. Aldo Leopold, "Wherefore Wildlife Ecology?" in *The River of the Mother of God and Other Essays by Aldo Leopold*, edited by Susan L. Flader and J. Baird Callicott (Madison: University of Wisconsin Press, 1991), 337.

13. Aldo Leopold, *Round River: From the Journals of Aldo Leopold*, ed. Luna B. Leopold (New York: Oxford University Press, 1953), 165.

maybe tragically, but to be helpless to do otherwise…To want the best for it…Desperately."[14]

But is the attachment that leads to engagement with the forces of diminishment and degradation—painful, frustrating, and discouraging as it so often is—a means of grace? To the extent it is successful, we can say that it makes *ourselves* a channel of grace for those places and their inhabitants. And it can also be a means of grace for us. In the words of Peter Forbes, Director of the Center for Land and People:

> Land conservation can tear down the walls that divide people from themselves, from one another, and from nature, and thus can become the starting point for a renewed community life. Conserving land can bring into people's moral universe a renewed sense of justice, meaning, respect, joy, and love, and make people feel more complete.[15]

The danger is that nostalgia and regret can turn to cynicism, bitterness, apathy on the one hand, or angry fanaticism on the other. Anxiety about the continued security and integrity of a place can reinforce the exclusivism and fortress mentality evoked by the container metaphor. Threats to existing patterns of life and relationship in a place are often seen as originating from the "outside"—particularly from strangers and immigrants—and this perception can give rise to brutal racism and nativism.

The internal structure of a place may itself be corrupted or dysfunctional, and may need to change. It may involve patterns of unjust and oppressive relationships among its members—classism, racism, or sexism. It may place excessive restrictions on individual freedom or block opportunities for self-fulfillment and self-expression, or the environmental or economic conditions for human life may be harsh and demanding, allowing for little more than the struggle to survive. After moving to Chicago, it did not take me long to realize what a deep hold the structures of institutionalized racism still have in this country—a fact that was easier to overlook (for me, at least) in an ethnically homogeneous community like Fargo. I can remember thinking, when I would take the train to the Loop to go to

---

14. Moore, 2.

15. Peter Forbes, "Saving Land and People" in *Ethics for a Small Planet: A Communications Handbook on the Ethical and Theological Reasons for Protecting Biodiversity* [italics, not underlined] (Madison, Wis.: The Biodiversity Project, 2002), 79.

the Art Institute or the Field Museum, that parts of some South Side neighborhoods looked like the aftermath of World War III.

The "place as constellation" metaphor has its virtues: it shifts attention from boundaries to interconnections and interactions, enabling an understanding of grace as the gift of life with and through particular others. Yet, it, too, can be problematic if it is taken to imply the limitation of affection and concern to proximate neighbors alone. Again, we seem to need another metaphor for place that can bring out the ways in which places and our attachment to them can mediate the resources of grace needed to counter these destructive ambiguities.

Place as Lens

The final metaphor I wish to examine is that of "place as lens," or focal point, which may help to overcome some of the limitations of the other two metaphors while pointing the way to a fuller sense of the grace of our attachments to places.

By "place as lens" I mean place as a node in a network of relationships. Just as a place is characterized by the relationships among the set of things within it, a place is also the nexus of a web of connections to the wider world. Places have always been characterized by interactions with their wider environment: their boundaries are always somewhat permeable. With the accelerating process of globalization, the scope and intensity of these interactions have increased by orders of magnitude. In a sense, this metaphor is an extension of the metaphor of place as a constellation or web of relationships: it extends the relationships that define a place beyond its boundaries.

The image of a lens suggests itself because of the way in which a lens gathers light or images from far away and brings them into focus at a particular spot. It thus unites the particularity of a point in space—a focal point or point of view—with a wide scope or field of attention. It is precisely as *this* focal point of *these* wider relationships that this place is what it is; it is in this place that these more distant realities become known and relevant, that these more general and abstract global phenomena become concrete and immediate. The lines of dependence which support us converge on this place; this place is also the point out from which our own lines of influence radiate out. A particular place is, in this understanding, an avenue or angle of approach into a much vaster web of relationships and influences. To know one's place is to understand it in its wider context of extended relationships. In the poet Richard Wilbur's phrase, a place is "a peculiar window on the whole."[16]

The context of a particular place is not only ecological, historical, economic, political, and so on: it is also a spiritual context. The "lens" metaphor illuminates the sacramental dimension of the grace of place: the wider horizon for which a particular place may serve as a "focal point" includes God's presence in and dealings with creation.

Perhaps the most obvious way in which this dimension is expressed is the idea of a "sacred place"—a place, where the presence of God, Spirit, the Holy, The Sacred, the Transcendent (whatever one wants to name it) is most strongly felt. In religious symbolism, such a place is often described as the *axis mundi*, the hub or center of the world where heaven and earth make contact. It is not necessarily a church or temple or other site explicitly defined as "religious." Wilderness areas have this character for many people, as may special, secluded spots in more familiar territory. It has often seemed to me that the Leopold "Shack" was a kind of a "sacred place" for Leopold and his family, and continues to play that role for many of his admirers—myself included—who have made their pilgrimages to it.

But this potentiality is not exclusively tied to fixed, specific locations; any place is potentially sacramental. As the angels sang in Isaiah's vision of the throne of God, "the whole earth is full of his glory." (Isa. 6:3, NRSV). And in the words of poet Gerard Manley Hopkins (whom Sittler never tired of quoting), "The world is charged with the grandeur of God." In the light of the cosmic scope of God's grace, a sharp distinction between "sacred" and "secular" places can hardly be sustained. Whatever place we may find ourselves in is a field for the operations of grace, and for our response to it.

For Christian faith, the paradigm for the manifestation of the Holy in a single point is the Incarnation of Christ. Sittler used the metaphor

---

16. Richard Wilbur, *Responses: Prose Pieces, 1953-1976* (New York: Harcourt Brace Jovanovich, 1976), 160.

of a "focal point" to describe the relationship between the "common grace" that fills creation and the "special grace" of Christ. The gospel of Christ is the focal *point* of grace, while the *region* of God's grace—the scope of the presence of grace—is "all that is, has been and will be," "not less than the whole creation."[17] It is also suggested by the hymn to Christ in the letter to the Colossians which declares Christ to be the one in whom "all things hold together" and in whom "the fullness of God was pleased to dwell." (Col. 1:17, 19). Whether he meant to or not, poet William Riley well expressed the paradox of Incarnation in his poem, "Dwelling": "only within limits is the infinite real."[18] The question of how the Incarnation as an event occurring at a particular time (about 2000 years ago) and in a particular place (Palestine) relates to our understandings of time, space, and place cannot be explored at any greater length here, but it is a significant one for a fully developed theology of place.[19]

A sacramental understanding of place highlights two aspects of grace that are crucial for the relationship between one's own place and all the other places of the Earth. The first aspect is universality: Grace is not just here or there—it is everywhere. No place is cut off from the grace of God that we have come to know in this place; and nowhere we can go can cut us off from that grace. The second is diversity: Grace is manifest not just in places like our own. Diverse places express diverse forms of goodness and giftedness. Sittler saw "diversity" as a key characteristic of the grace of creation:

> Grace comes in colors…[this understanding of grace] is bound up with the unthinkable variety of God the creator who loves all colors, textures, forms, nuances, and modes of life. It is grace as the joyful acknowledgment of the variety that God loves, the variety he has made.[20]

---

17. Sittler, "Excerpts from *Essays on Nature and Grace*," in *Evocations of Grace*, 153-54.

18. Northwest Earth Institute, *Discussion Course on Discovering a Sense of Place* (Portland, Ore.: The Institute, 2001), I-3.

19. See discussions in Lilburne, and in H. Paul Santmire, "So That He Might Fill All Things: Comprehending the Cosmic Love of Christ.", *Dialog: A Journal of Theology* (forthcoming).

20. Sittler, "Ecological Commitment as Theological Responsibility" in *Evocations of Grace*, 86.

To expand our understanding of the grace of place-attachment as that is illuminated by the place-as-lens metaphor, we need to work with a more explicitly dynamic definition of grace than we have been using so far. Sittler set forth such a dynamic understanding of grace: "By grace is meant all that God does to crack nature [including human nature] open to its God, to restore it to his love and to its intended destiny."[21] To put it in terms less vivid but still useful for our purpose, *Grace is God's free and loving action in and toward the creation by which creation and its creatures are upheld, transformed, and directed toward God's intended fulfillment of creation.*

How is God's gracious purpose for creation worked out through our attachment to a place or places? Attachment to place can be a means of grace as through it God transforms and calls us to fulfill our role in God's purposes for creation in whatever place we are set. Loyalty to one's particular place is part of the meaning of attachment. How does our loyalty in and to our own place serve as a focal point for the wider cause of the God's transforming grace in and for creation?

At least a major aspect of the "human vocation"—our role in the divine purpose for creation insofar as we are human—is the care of the earth. In the second chapter of Genesis we read that the first human being was created from the dust of the earth and placed in the Garden of Eden to "till it and keep it" (Gen. 2:15). A more literal translation would be "to *serve* it and keep it." The human being, it would seem, is created for the earth, rather than the other way around, for the text states that the earth at first was barren because there was neither rain to water it, nor anyone to cultivate it (Gen. 2:5).

Thus the care of the earth, which is both a source of profound joy for people (though, to be sure, a source of pain and frustration as well) and a means to the well-being of both people and nature, is also the glorification God, for it allows the glory of God to shine forth more fully from the created world, and the grace of God to be more fully and richly enjoyed by God's creatures.

Since we only encounter creation concretely in particular places, our serving and keeping of creation can only happen in and to

---

21. Sittler, "Commencement Address" in *Evocations of Grace*, 35.

particular places. Thus, to carry out our earth-keeping task means to appreciate, understand, defend and enhance particular places within the creation—especially, but not exclusively, the places where we ourselves live and work and play—and through them to enhance the rich and diverse tapestry of the planet. Our places—our "Edens" if you will—are delivered into our care for the glory of God; and this glory is manifested not in humanity alone or in nature alone, but in the symbiotic relationship between them, which is enacted not in creation-in-general, but in particular places. Thus, God's glory is reflected and refracted in the "unthinkable variety" of the diversity of human-place symbioses as these are found in particular places. Having lived in Midwestern communities ranging from the bucolic countryside of rural Wisconsin to the affluent and academic enclave of the Hyde Park neighborhood on the South Side of Chicago, I have learned that each type of landscape combines nature and culture in a way that is capable of glorifying God. However far short it may fall of realizing its potential, each offers a unique glimpse of what a flourishing creation *could* be like.

At the same time, our sense of responsibility and concern must reach out to the wider world: Because of the network of economic, political and ecological relationships within which our own place is embedded, we cannot ignore the global context. What we do in our local communities contributes to national and global problems. Likewise, these global problems have local impacts that threaten the character of the particular places where we live, work, and enjoy creation's beauty and integrity.

Human-induced climate change provides one of the clearest examples of this interdependence between local and global issues. Simply by virtue of being Americans, I and my neighbors are among the greatest contributors to the problem. The U.S. is by far the largest emitter of greenhouse gases (mostly produced by the burning of fossil fuels) which are believed to create a heat-trapping "blanket" around the earth. The Union of Concerned Scientists and the Ecological Society of America have produced a report detailing projected impacts of climate change on the Great Lakes region. The report makes clear that, in addition to its consequences for human health, agriculture, property, and infrastructure, climate change can severely impact the things that make our places special. In Wisconsin, for example, the climate is likely to grow warmer and drier during this century, altering the ecosystems of lakes, rivers, fish, wetlands and northern forests. The report notes that warmer winters will disrupt the forms of winter recreation, like skiing, snowmobiling, ice fishing, that are "an integral part of people's sense of place" in this state."[22]

Yet even the more distant consequences of our actions are felt, not by a generalized "global environment" or abstract "humanity," but by other particular places and people. The brunt of climate change will be borne by developing nations such as Bangladesh: poor, and with a quarter of its densely populated land less than three meters above sea level, it is especially vulnerable to the increased flooding, storm surges and sea level rise that are expected to come with global warming.[23]

Many states and even local communities are taking the initiative to reduce their own contribution to climate change. In July, 2003, ten northeast states came together to develop a regional strategy to address climate change. Madison, Wisconsin, has developed a "Climate Protection Plan," joining over 290 other cities in a Cities for Climate Protection Campaign. Individual state or city efforts do seem unequal to the scope of the problem. But any solution will be, at bottom, the sum total of local changes in the way we produce and use energy. Even national initiatives and international mechanisms and agreements can only encourage, enable, or require such changes.

PLACE AND PATRIOTISM

In the light of preceding discussion, we can now return to Sittler's comments connecting the grace of attachment to place with "patriotism." What do we mean by "patriotism?" The simple, conventional definition of patriotism is "love of country." But what do we mean by "country"?

It is striking that when Sittler speaks of what America "is" he does not refer to abstract ideas such as "democracy," "liberty," or "the spirit of enterprise." Rather, he describes it as a kind of patchwork of places:

---

22. www.uscusa.org/greatlakes/pdf/wisconsin.pdf
23. Donald A. Brown, *American Heat: Ethical Problems with the United States' Response to Global Warming* (Lanham Maryland: Rowman and Littlefield, 2002), 92-93.

Have you who read these lines never gone inwardly a-wandering among the myriad impacts of this magnificent land?—the sprawling, opulent south, she of the stark red earth and the blithe and lazy skies; the tragic, lonely beauty of New England, her neat white houses and her stone fences, so proper to her prim certainty; the sweep of the middle west with her little towns set astride ten thousand main streets that become white concrete ribbons that stretch or curve across the countryside of incredible fertility and scope; the terrible distances of the western states where farmer's families of a Saturday night "run into town"—eighty miles!—with insouciant ease; and the fabulous west coast, majestic at the top where Rainier sparkles, rich and worldly-wise at the center where the land enfolds in long arms the lovely bay, and the fantastic glitter and brashness at the bottom where sprawls and brawls the city of the angels![24]

Similarly, the America Leopold knew and loved was a more concrete reality than the "land" extolled by many of his "patriotic" contemporaries:

…Do we not already sing our love for and obligation to the land of the free and the home of the brave? Yes, but just what and whom do we love? Certainly not the soil, which we are sending helter-skelter downriver. Certainly not the waters, which we assume have no function except to turn turbines, float barges, or carry off sewage. Certainly not the plants, of which we exterminate whole communities without batting an eye. Certainly not the animals, of which we have already extirpated many of the largest and most beautiful species.[25]

In terms of the metaphor of "place as lens," one's country is the focal point of a web of relationships that links us to those beyond its spatially defined limits. Our relationship to our country thus has two sides: It is a larger "place" to which we are related through our relationship to more intimate, local places, and it is also a place which finds it full meaning and significance in its relationship to the wider world.

And what do we mean by "love"?

As we have seen, love of place—including love of country— is a grace whereby we acknowledge our belonging to our place as both a gift and an opening of ourselves in response to something beyond not only our selves but also our place or nation: namely, the grace and glory of God

---

24. Sittler, "Grace Note," 3.
25. Leopold, *Sand County Almanac*, 204.

in and for the creation. It is therefore not a love that is curved inward upon itself, limited by its own walls or borders, but one that reaches out in solidarity to other places and accepts responsibility for the impacts that its actions may have on its near or distant neighbors. It extends hospitality to the stranger and guest, and rejoices in the variety of gifts born of diverse places with their distinctive landscapes and cultures.

Nor is such love blind and uncritical of the places to which it is attached. Patriotism is often equated with unconditional affirmation of anything done in the name of the honor, defense, or prosperity of the nation. But the same larger cause that may be served and embodied through a particular nation also stands in judgment over that nation. Sittler described the Christian stance toward the world as a kind of love-hate relationship:

> Because we are creatures of grace, we are not and never can identify our being with our existence, we cannot be at final rest within nature. But because we are creatures of nature, too, we must incarnate, actualize, in the solid stuff of concrete decisions and actions the powerful but unpredictable movements of God's relentless grace. This means that God's people in the earth must learn so to relate grace and nature as to love the world without idolatry and to hate the world without despair. One must hate the world enough to wish to change it; but he must love it enough to think it worth changing."[26]

A better way of formulating this stance may be that of Douglas John Hall, who expresses it as a paradoxical combination of love and judgment.[27] If this is the proper stance toward "the world" then it would seem to apply just as well to particular places within the world, including countries.

These two ideas—that one's country is a lens for one's relationships of responsibility and solidarity with the wider world; and that the proper stance toward one's country is one of critical love—may help us to understand Sittler's assertion that "true patriotism" does not necessarily lead to "arrogant nationalism," a "love" of one's own land that breeds contempt for other lands.

---

26. Joseph Sittler, "The Wood's in Trouble," *Discourse: A Review of the Liberal Arts* 1 (July 1950), 145.

27. Hall, *Imaging God*, 36ff.

> Loving, personal identification with one's own land has never been a breeder of arrogant nationalism. That would seem to be the logical result, but it isn't. For a man's love for his own land is the practical and earthy ground for respect for other men's love of their land. Just as he who has convictions alone knows the meaning of tolerance, so he alone can assess at right value the land-loves of other people who knows and deeply loves his own.[28]

A "patriotism" that is insular and uncritical is not an adequate love of homeland, for it does not do justice to its place. It does not recognize the full reality of that place as a node in a web that connects it to the holy fount of its graces and the divine criterion of its behavior, and that links it to other places which also stand in their own relation to the transforming love and judgment of God. It fails to connect that homeland vertically to its source in God and horizontally to the rest of creation.

Our love and loyalty for our own country is both affirmed and judged by the manner in which that loyalty does, or does not, give due regard to the good of places other than our own. As Lloyd Stone expressed it in a hymn written in the 1930's (to the tune of "Finlandia"):

> My country's skies are bluer than the ocean,
> and sunlight beams on cloverleaf and pine;
> But other lands have sunlight too, and clover,
> and skies are everywhere as blue as mine.[29]

But the qualities of attachment to place illuminated by the container and constellation metaphors are also needed to sustain a responsible place-based patriotism. The pitfalls of the "place as lens" metaphor include a danger that the ability to see and act beyond the limits of local boundaries and relationships can encourage an overestimation of one's power and knowledge and the temptation to assume that one's own interests are also the interests of the whole. A sense of national responsibility in and for the wider world can overcome isolationism and xenophobic defensiveness only to become a crusading, messianic nationalism that tries to remake the rest of the world into one's own image. The attitudes of humility, restraint, and keeping one's own

---

28. Sittler, "Grace Note," 3.
29. Lloyd Stone, "This Is My Song," *The New Century Hymnal* (Cleveland, Ohio: The Pilgrim Press, 1995), Hymn 591.

household in order that are encouraged by the more "parochial" metaphors of place can act as a necessary counterweight to those tendencies.

CONCLUSION: "WHERE ARE YOU RIGHT AT THIS MOMENT?"

One recent event embodies for me the sum and substance of these reflections. It underscores how the question with which I began this essay is an important one—but is not as simply answered as one might think. The date was Sunday, April 13, 2003, and the place was outside a church on the west side of Madison.

It was the evening of Palm Sunday. The hillside prairie plantings between the parking lot and the street had been burned during the preceding week. The land was covered with a layer of ash and patches of singed grass, a powerful image of desolation. But beneath the scorched earth, roots untouched by the flames lay waiting to send up new shoots through the charred surface. Soon the ground would be covered with a green haze of new growth, and by midsummer it would be thick with tall prairie grasses, yellow and purple coneflowers, and bergamot.

Prairie restoration projects are common in Madison and southern Wisconsin, and in many ways are emblematic of the ecological conscience of the area. Curtis Prairie, in the University of Wisconsin Arboretum in Madison (where Leopold, incidentally, served as director of animal research), is the oldest restored prairie in the world, and was the "laboratory" where the role of fire in maintaining prairie ecosystems was discovered. Throughout the city, in yards and on city property, are patches of prairie plants—not all of which constitute "restored" prairies, but which are at least gestures in the direction of restoration. They are both a way of honoring and remembering the tallgrass prairies that once covered the heart of the North American continent—of which only about 5% remain—and tokens of hope for a more viable symbiosis between human beings and nature. This particular project (itself not yet a fully successful restoration), like the newly-installed photovoltaic solar panels on the church roof, is a witness that the care of the earth is an essential part of the Christian faith.

On the crest of the hill in the midst of the burned prairie stood seven crosses, representing those killed in the attacks on the World Trade Center and the Pentagon, and in Afghanistan. Behind them, a banner reading "The Human Cost of This War." The war in Iraq had begun shortly before. This was the site of an evening service, for which more than 100 persons had gathered. Following a reading from Lamentations, prayers of sorrow, and a solo, "By Babylonian Waters," participants stepped onto the scorched ground with stones, hammers and simple crosses. They placed the stones on the ground and pounded the crosses into the dirt to commemorate the American, British, and Iraqi lives lost, both soldiers and civilians. (Stones were used as well as crosses because rocks are used in Iraq to mark graves.) The silence was punctuated only by the blows of the hammers and the beating of a single drum as some 900 crosses were planted; at that time, the casualties of the war numbered in the thousands. After more hymns, prayers, and scripture readings, all left in silence in the gathering dusk.

All this was, of course, controversial. The pastor of the church received about a dozen angry calls from non-parishioners. Many saw it as an unpatriotic anti-war protest, or an inappropriate mixing of politics and religion. Some pointed—quite justly—to the thousands of victims of Saddam Hussein's horrifyingly brutal dictatorship. (None, however, were interested in discussing the issues raised, or in adding markers to represent those victims.)

While it can't be denied that the crosses were meant to raise questions about the means and ends of U.S. actions and the prevailing euphoria at the war's progress, it would be a mistake to see that as the only, or even the primary, meaning of the event. Justified or not, "successful" or not, war is always a tragedy. It is all to easy to forget that fact when that war occurs somewhere else, with relatively little cost to one's own side, and with few hardships felt at home.

In terms of the above analysis, the constellation of things gathered together at that time and constituting that place—the people, the burned prairie, the smell of ashes and the sound of the drum and hammers borne on the wind, the rocks and crosses, the evening light falling on everything—pointed beyond the walls of their "containers," city limits and national borders, and became a lens focusing our hearts and minds on the pain of a distant land, and on the groaning and travailing of the whole creation.

What was the grace there? Certainly there was grace in the promise of resurrection foreshadowed by the crosses and symbolized by the green life coiled and waiting like a spring in the prairie soil. But another dimension of grace was there as well. In the words of H. Richard Niebuhr's essay "War as Crucifixion," written during World War II:

> Yet how the divine grace appears in the crucifixion of war may become somewhat clear when the cross of Christ is used to interpret it. Then our attention is directed to the death of the guiltless, the gracious, and the suffering of the innocent becomes a call to repentance, to a total revolution of our minds and hearts. And such a call to repentance—not to sorrow but to spiritual revolution—is an act of grace, a great recall from the road to death which we all travel together, the just and the unjust, the victors and the vanquished.[30]

And as the blackened hillside reminded us, nature, too, is one of the victims of war. (Saddam Hussein's military campaign against insurgents during the 1990's drained the marshes along the Iran-Iraq border—one of the world's greatest environmental disasters, and devastating to the "marsh Arabs" and their culture.)

It seems to be a simple question: *Where are you at this very moment?*

The simple answer: On a plot of burned prairie in Madison, Wisconsin, April 13, 2003. But reflected in the multiple facets of this singular time and place are other places, other times: Bloody Iraq. Devastated Afghanistan. Shattered New York. Darkened Golgotha. The epoch of the great tallgrass prairies, before white settlement. Passover, sometime around 30 AD. Sometime, perhaps, in the indefinite future of wars and rumors of war.

Like a receiver catching signals bounced from an orbiting satellite, this place connects me to those places through its connection to the One who draws together all times, all places: the Creator, Judge and Redeemer of the Earth—the source, circumference, and center of the world.

---

30. H. Richard Niebuhr, "War as Crucifixion," *The Christian Century* (April 28, 1943), 515.

Peter Bakken
Research Fellow
Au Sable Institute of Environmental Studies

I was born and raised in Fargo, North Dakota and currently live in Madison, Wisconsin with my wife, daughter and three cats. We enjoy reading, playing games, and going on walks and outings together. We are members of the Evangelical Lutheran Church in America. My dissertation was titled "The Ecology of Grace: Ultimacy and Environmental Ethics in Aldo Leopold and Joseph Sittler." I was a member of the task force that produced the E.L.C.A. social statement, "Caring for Creation: Vision, Hope and Justice." My publications include *Ecology, Justice and Christian Faith: A Critical Guide to the Literature* (co-compiled with J. Ronald Engel and Joan Gibb Engel; Greenwood Press, 1995) and *Evocations of Grace: Writings on Ecology, Theology and Ethics by Joseph Sittler* (co-edited with Steven Bouma-Prediger).

Roadscapes: Central USA
Poetry by Nancy Adams-Cogan

Photo Ed Heffron

I grew up among the pines and plentiful shores of Michigan's Upper Peninsula, truly and visually immersed in lakes of all sizes. I have lived and learned in eastern and Midwestern states, except for a year of seminary in Berkeley, California. Most of my years have been spent in caring for a family of eight, and teaching in public school and Head Start speech and language programs. I am now a hospital chaplain, specializing in geriatric care, and writing poem portraits of my elders.

Many of my occupations have required driving through open country in varied weathers and seasons, usually alone. Unable to point out and comment upon what attracted my attention, I took to writing as I drove, on a yellow pad or an envelope beside me on the seat. Against the wisest advice, I continue to record what I see, how I think and feel about it. Sometimes, I can read the words later and develop a poem. No vehicle accidents have yet occurred! Only minor collisions of observation, paper, pencil and imaginal response.

Standing always in the center of my own circular world, sensing, interpreting, conversing, making some meaning of experiences, I am always learning, always informed by then and there. As I am, I am here now.

ARABESQUES ON BLACKTOP

Trees waltz along the way
Turning in the corner of my eye
Caught as I drive by.

A pair of maples dancing
Fit the beat and melody
Of Strauss on air.
One fine beginning for a day;
Poplars contradance in rows.
Getting to work is play.

ON DRIVING ON
(or What Now into Then What)

This road climbs
Drops and twists;
I see only where I am
Now to the next turn
The top of the next rise.
I know where I have been
But cannot tell it out
Straight and plumb.

In pickup trucks I meet
Waving strangers greet me;
I reciprocate because
I am right here.
We share this time,
This momentary
  space link.

I am here,
I am moving on,
And I am now
  Letting go of then
  and there…

PORCINE AURICLES PORCELAINE

Have you ever
seen a small white pig
prisoned by wire
in the shadowed cleft
between two looming
scarlet barns?

The young pig waiting
shifts, is now imperially
crowned by early morning
sunbeams;

Its brief gaudy aura gleams
in royal rose and gold
through the finest of
translucent
ears.

COUNTRY ROAD DEVOTIONS

Speeding along
the rumpled dark grey ribbon of
this country road

orchards houses fencerows barns

engage my eye
flash past and disappear
as rolling Iowa hills roll over them
then surface too late to be
held again in sight and mind

attractions bygones left behind

Seeking signs of You
in the landscape passing
I climb and coast and climb again
attempting connection
        Creator of Universes
but
distracted by a sudden truck
slowing to steer blindly around
a combine creeping far
too near the edge

then barely missing
        thank you, Lord of All,
that arrogant fowl
roostering splendidly again today
onto the blacktop

I just drive
until

clear long views coming
I can leave a little fear in charge
of routine caution and direction
to sink and seek again in words
nearing center
    Lord Jesus Christ
    Son of God
        Savior
        Have mercy on me
           a sinner
and I know
pure Being lives
within beyond around
me still connecting
all that is

A LAPSED FARM

The house
has skeleton and skin,
through mouth or other orifice
a broken window, missing board
or door ajar, allows invasion
by passing eyes.

Abandoned
it stands beside the road
machine shed fallen in, barn going down
surrounded by fenceless corn and bean fields;
hedgerows and family long gone it stands alone
its bare wood skin shrinks and separates
permitting access to the contents
of sitting room and kitchen
their artifacts deserted
by departed lives.

On my way
saddened and curious
each day my eyes pursue
a glimpse of weathered chairs
one rocked by wind, torn shades.
Tattered calendars emptied frames
hint at what is hidden there
in closet or in cellar left
for me to know
not ever.

Still I see
flames of day lilies spread
white peony bushes persisting
circles of iris purpling the slope
a subtle rabbit crops red
clover on former lawn
as I move on.

Sic Transit
Gloria Mundi
for all who pass
this way

I AND COW

Driving into sunrise
on a late winter morn
observe a cow alone
among a herd the one
wading into a farm pond
knee deep in its icy water
barely thawing into spring

and passing feel the chill
invading arms and legs as
though you were standing
four-leggedly on hooves

yourself within her russet hide
hipbones prominent in haunches
brow bovine lowering too soon
into shattering surface reflecting bits
of browngold eyes flaring nostrils
topknot velvet ears and horns

then feel the coldness fast
fade out of flesh and bone
one intimate invasion
of another being
past

drive on
enriched by a moment
transformed and new
returned to body

offer thanks
for the gift of
a verging cow
forever now
within.

THE RIVERS OF IOWA

Who owns
the rivers of Iowa
waters of The Beautiful Land?

The Cedar, the Iowa
The Wapsipinicon

The Rock and the Turkey
Little Sioux, Racoon
and Chariton

The Shell Rock and the Floyd
Upper Iowa, Maquoketa
Little Cedar
Big Sioux

North River
Middle River
South River, too

DesMoines
West and East Fork
Maple, Walnut
English

Nishnabotna
Boyer and Skunk
Nodaway East
Nodaway West

Last, not least,
First, not best

Big Mississippi east
Wide Missouri west
Impoundments, lakes
and all the rest

Indian Creek
A thousand creeks
Running every which way
Feed all the rivers
Into flowing.

Who owns
The rivers of Iowa?
Their rushing waters,
Broad floodplains,
Green banks?

Their fish and turtles,
Frogs and floating joy?
Who owns the waters?
How and
Why?

MIDSUMMER MASSES

No church for us today, Lord.
Enroute to a gathering of friends,
  we worship with our eyes wide
  open to profusions of lavender pink
  oswego tea exploding softly
  among sown patches of crown vetch,
  flocks of yellow birdfoot trefoil.
Your glory borders the way.

Day lilies miraculously massed
  in well tended congregations
  or fiercely independent thrive
  mirror the sultry sun
in sacred celebration.

Wild chicory
  flowers sparsely on each stalk
  reflects high heaven's hue
  fills passing fields to overflowing
  with tattered snips of clear ethereal blue
  proferred for ravenous review.
We keep the feast.

Make these visions ours forever,
Gracious Lord, and keep us
ever wondering.

Love, dwell in us
as in the beauty of your world.

Amen Amen
ALLELUIA

EMBROIDER THESE

Twelve covered box carriages beyond Lancaster
Rows of black silhouettes cross farmyards,
Travel at the edge of public roads.

Pheasants, lambs and piglets
Calves, foals and blooming trees appear
in the border counties.

The rear window of my wagon
Opens onto soft evening sunset
Glowing rose on silvered puddles.

Groves are carpeted with wild ecstatic blue,
Sown rows of sweet domesticated blossoms
Blown by southeast breezes.

Three golden does arranged
On a field of dusky green,
Not one fawn to be seen.

One hawk skims beneath the power lines
Toward a warm supper of mouseflesh.
Hidden in lavender oswego tea.

Deep brown stretches to pale cerulean sky and silver clouds,
Becoming pink-tinged on a horizon line patterned
With darkly figured trees, a barn, a house and horses.

Work them all with needles flashing
Anchoring your rainbow flosses on clean linen;
Keep them ever present for hungry eyes and memory,
Set out in satin, bouillon, herringbone and chain.

EROS AND RETURNING HOME

Always when I must be going
shadows of my early self remain here
in memory of fernhomes and forest floors
dim cathedral spaces of pine woods where
my mind wanders among rough pillars as dreams
fall on needles softly carpeting the sand with rust
or strays along a stand of sapling maples
winter bare, new-leafed or flaming
seasonal as my soul.

Ends of my heartstrings seem
to be embedded in granite outeroppings
in rock cuts created by the roads I must travel
to leave my birthplace, and its red dust, inscribed
ledges, clumps of daisy, yellow buttercup and
orange paintbrush set beneath the bluest sky
strike hard, evoke old yearning to stay here,
invoke new tears with each new wrenching
of sark from sacred ground.

II.
Many years ago not far away
the girl wished for her own vision
imagined meeting a black bear on the path
made connection with a greater wildness
and told stories of her sightings never too near,
always thrilling never real enough to harm.

At the darker edge of mind
the shape of a bear remains to haunt me;
the moon of deep desire growing summons
my absent body flowing into dreamscapes,
silver moon light quivering on lakes
shadows sliding into forest.

Always a sliver in my soul
longs for contact with the bear
belonging to a home I can
no longer claim as mine
in choosing exile,

Imagines kindly eyes
furred paws passing weighted
over cool pale skin caressing claws
heat transmitting feral welcome
courting reluctant synapses into
a passionate response I want
and do not want
to own.

Wildness reaches
into the turned black earth
of my dreaming body
joy touches eros revives
its most material being.

III.
Old collisions past recalling
pierce each passing moment
of engagement and release
create sensations of encounter
far beyond what can be seen

Suggest encounters ancient as
the ever-changing inland sea
lifetimes of rifts to be resolved
and dangerous embraces.

IV.
Bear Spirit,
in the running waves
and the wind waves
molding fine sand
scattering stones

on inland seashores
I can feel within
you are,

In bark and branch
leaf needle blossom
cone and fruit of trees
you are,

Coloring my dreams
of going home to an arc of sky
to heights of azure blue
domes of granite grey
clouds passing,

Everywhere
for better
for worse
you are

The bear desired
as a fiercer part of me
the shape of a bear
drawn in woodsmoke
on the ochre walls
of a cave lining
my wild soul.

THESE TREES

What have these trees to do with me?
Trees that bloom and fade and leaf along my way
Trees I look upon with regularity.

Anticipation whets my eye;
My trees stand branch to branch in groves

Or stark against the stretching sky,
Alone in lonely silhouette.

Greedy, I seek them;
My gaze leaps out to feast on hope,
Assessing health and growth,
Buds opening, leaves glowing,

In all ways beautiful to see.
What have these trees to do
With me?

A WILD TURKEY WAS IT

> I only wanted to stare myself into him
> to try and Thou him till we recognized
> and became each other.
> —Isabella Gardner (and a heron)

On the first day of turkey hunting season, I was about to leave the MFA station after checkup, change of fluids and amiable conversation, my old station wagon and my mood in better repair. I paused inside the door as several hunters swarmed through to surround the counter, choosing candy bars and plug to chew, comparing notes on the morning's strategy, locations and armaments. Recalling years when I had ritually hidden my BAMBI books from my father to keep him from finding deer when he went off to deer camp, I made mental notes, as I listened, about this new killing time. What must local turkeys know about these louts in order to stay alive?

Tiring of their predatory banter and my own predictable response, I pushed through the door and stepped into brisk golden air. Settling into the driver's seat of my Country Sedan for Nine, I started her engine and pulled up out of the dusty lot onto the blacktop. My Elizabeth Ford Wagonner's big body closed around me like a private shell, a coach provided to carry me along in life. She was one solid daily remnant of my marriage, which had run well for over twenty eight years, then suddenly stopped with my husband's heart. When this old ship of the road sank I would have to look for something smaller and more economical-but this big mama was all paid for and all mine. I could lock the doors and sleep inside her—if I could get away.

Distributing my time and energy to part-time jobs, good causes, and relationships about which I cared passionately was leaving me depleted. Not much changed; not much came back to me. "Patroness of Lost Causes" my husband had called me. Now that he was gone, I wanted my connections and yet I wanted out of everything. I could not seem to complete projects or keep reluctant promises, but just trailed off into minimal responses to the next call for letters or focused attention. Like the sharp-faced woman in a Jules Feiffer cartoon long carried in my mind, I had taken to murmuring, "They'll never get me alive." I wanted the past to be present, but everything was changing. Sailing alone along the highway should give me time to contemplate a new life. I did not.

Crossing the Chariton River, climbing the long grade on the other side, I drove toward home, toward bills, tuition notices, phone messages, plaintive letters from worthy causes, books begging to be read and Things To Do, waiting to be prioritized and sorted into A, B, C or D lists. Paper tasks, paper people! Just paper! And there were the grown children I could not comfort and a thirteen year old daughter, who had been hit hardest by her father's sudden death. Through a grey fogbank of sorrows I kept on driving.

Passing the meadow where I always looked for wild turkeys, I checked the corner of my eye. No turkey shapes today. Perhaps they knew what day this was, and had already trotted off to hide in secret ancestral turkey retreats, until being seen would be safer. Though I relished catching their ungainly bodies in sight, I hoped they really had gone to ground for the hunting season. There was some comfort in the time limits lowered by law around those hungry gunsights. Perhaps the killing time could come and then go for turkeys.

Immersed for a mile or two in musing on the lives and deaths of turkeys and of men, on dangers lurking inside their bodies, as well as in the world, I nearly missed the line of dark birdforms turkeying up a sloping meadow toward the deserted Girl Scout camp on the ridge. Following them with my eyes, I slowed the wagon, seized by a desire to keep them, always present on demand. My camera was in my backpack and I knew the camp road would intersect their path. I could park outside the gate and approach the flock on its familiar ruts.

Turning quickly off the new highway into a leftover segment of the old way, I turned sharply left again, stopped at a metal gate. Taking the camera from its case. I closed the car door with care, climbed through the wire fence beside the gate, and padded toward the place on the road where I expected the turkeys to cross.

Like a guilty thing surprised, I startled when they appeared at a nearer point and turned toward me in the sandy tracks. Wishing I were closer and ready to shoot, I labored hard at moving nothing. Barely breathing,

I watched as they waddled on, stopping for a moment to inspect the ground beneath their feet, then approaching, unaware of me. I wished that I knew more about appearing acceptable to turkeys; I wished that I had frozen with lens and shutter oriented to fix them forever as they ran. It was too late to catch them unaware on film, but if I could just resist the desire to snap or even to blink, surely they would come closer.

I waited…hoping…but somehow they knew. All but one turned aside, running into the woods. That lone bird wandered on, head bobbing, searching through dry grass yellowing on the median. Oblivious to warnings cranked out by its fellows, it lifted its head, riffled shining feathers, moved closer and still closer. I could not breathe, my chest bound by intense longing for connection with this silly bird. "Look at me," I called out silently.

Lines from the poet Isabella Gardner, written in response to Martin Buber's I AND THOU, slithered into my mind. In her poem she pursued a heron, attempting to meet its eye.

> I only wanted to stare myself into him, to try and Thou him
> till we recognized and became each other.

For the merest moment this turkey's gaze brushed mine, but summoned once again by anxious gobbling behind, it moved off the track to join its tribe in flight. "I couldn't shoot you! I would never hurt you," I shouted after it in frustration. It was gone.

Left with neither image on film nor sense of connection, I realized the transience of the encounter, now past and subject to the vagaries of memory. Even a stupid turkey could not be converted into Thou, but would be IT. I could not preserve it from gunshots, call it family, even give it space on a page in the family album. I turned away.

I snapped several branches of brilliantly vermillion leaves, remaining bold against cerulean sky, then tucked the camera into my backpack. It was a short hike to the car; satisfied for the moment, I drove away toward my emptying house.

DRIVING EAST

At dawn I saw
wild turkeys fly.

They ran a few steps
then rose
airborne ungainly
like dirigibles

astounding wings
outstretched
to carry them
all fearful
all wonderfully
made
away

from sudden jeopardy
on barren blacktop,
from exploration
of its emptiness
now broken,

into sanctuaries
of thickets leading back
and back into encircling
forest depths of life—
no death by car
today

I am renewed
by clumsy
but heroic flight,
wise exodus from
a dark road into
hickory-filtered
light.

ILLUMINATED TEXT

Tense,
clenched,
driving mile
after mile through
a drizzly night under
the darkest phase
of moon
I am

Startled by
a sudden gift
a cloud of fireflies
surrounds the shell
of my good wagon.
They light my sight
then fall away
behind

And I return
to pondering as I go
abstracts of Godness
on the yellowed tablets
of inherited mindsets
rewriting Thee
and Thou
enroute.

Rejecting old address
forms for a Divine Patriarch
far off somewhere in space
and the rules for praying
properly that rise from
deepset roots of fear
disguised as hope,

I know
that Love is
Light breathing.
The road is dark
but the moon
rises.

AN EYE FOR ENTROPY

1.
Crossing the state
on the same highways
several times in each season
leads to closer observation

In a roaming mind of features,
artifacts and new constructions,
oak trees, beanfields, buildings
seen repeatedly in transit.

2.
Qualities of caressing light alter
from midday white to late day amber;
seasonal contexts are transformed
from leaves to leafless to leafing,
Bent brown weeds proceed
through stages of collapse.

Farmsteads given to decay
occupy niches in expectation,
so that I look for them enroute
and want them not to be gone.
In a town one '48 Kaiser nestles
in plumed grass beside a house,

Empty with shattered panes,
lost shingles, one hanging door,
deteriorating slowly, its peaked
roof sagging toward ground.

3.
A small cornpicker dragon
looks back toward burning flights,

long retired from forays after treasure,
rusts at home in its own green valley.

Further down the road brush grows
over a junked Chevy; branches invade
its stripped interior stopped only by
perpetual lack of sunbeams.

4.
Now the weathered corncrib stands
no longer before the barn, no longer shows
its open face to the road, having gone perhaps
to fill some fast eroding ditch;

Like trees dying, falling into earth
buildings, vehicles, tools return.
Attention must be paid.

ACCOUNTS RECEIVABLE: ROADKILL

Driving home
one counts
and regrets each
new roadkill.

Too many
raccoons rest
four feet uplifted
ballooning forms intact
along the edge of blacktop

And fetus-like
a tailed and tiny
body rolls dead
along the yellow
centerlines.

Stilled dabs of squirrel
wind-ruffled tails
of skunks and cats
comprise the body
count today,

Dashing, dying, rotting
feeding vultures.

Lessons abound here
questions resound about
disparities in ownership
property rights intrusive
cross purposes colliding;
Land rights create on earth
long swaths of sacred space
preserved for wheels to speed
from point to point, to cut across
wild freedom and free creatures

Dashing, dying, rotting
feeding crows

Past fields of grazing stock held safely
caught within borders of fencepost and wire
for later consumption,   now consuming
meadow grass and last year's corn.

Confess, repent
drive on with care
and terror.

Odebolt
(11/4/01)

In western Iowa
late in a mild autumn,
at Odebolt a heap of corn
stands high between highway
and railroad tracks. The corn waits

Not in the fields
but harvested, gathered
on the ground in Odebolt
where the elevators are full
the promise of corn lies waiting

For an attractive price
per bushel to come along
for a buyer and railroad transport;
an embarassing abundance of corn
waits for the next step.

While in Afghanistan
around the globe of earth
bitter winds of winter rush
through high mountain passes
snow covers decimated fields

Covers moutain strongholds
and camps crowded with displaced
persons, refugee families unsheltered;
while hunger is devouring souls
and bodies
hope for food is thinning.

What threads connect
the hungry and the crop?
What actions can be taken by whom
to replace emptiness and failing life
with western Iowa corn and energy?

Not simple you say?
Then make it so! Weave
the ethical and the economic
and the heart of Love
into compassion
acting...

ORDINARY BEAUTIES

TRITE
to contemplate
through a high window
brushwork of maple branches
drawing grey-brown lines
against a blue blue sky

or to adore
a sunset's crimson splendor
spread across the ruffled surfaces
of puddles as we pass by?

TRITE
to track the patterns
laid long by vapor trails
across the top of heaven

morphing into cloudforms
edges fuzzing catching lightroses
tones overlaid and fading?

TRITE
to appreciate the ordinary gifts
of morning and of evening light,
stars studding the darkest blue
of night awaiting moon,

to be recaptured daily by
the same old elements in view
hues and arrangements altering slightly
through every course of sun?

TRITE
perhaps to write but
not to notice not to offer
silent hymns to very ordinary
beauties?

WRITE.
Blessed be
and know
yourself
to be
so.

A GREENING PRAYER

Godde
keep me always
greening

keep me rooted
in the dark
keep me turning
to the light

keep me well
and deeply watered
keep me bending
with the winds

keep me growing
beyond fences
keep me leafing
budding blooming

keep me fruiting
keep me yielding
ever blessing
everything

keep me healing
calm and able
keep me still as
stillness calls

keep me always
greening
Godde

Blessing me just as I am,
Each new day blessing what I do
Incline my heart into your ways of love

AMEN AMEN
LET IT BE SO

MIDWESTERN ROADSCAPES
Photography by Rod Strampe

I am the center of my world…

I have always had a fascination with the contrast between light and shadow, and how it plays on different subjects. Equally fascinating to me is how a small change in perspective can so radically change the power and the message that an image delivers to the viewer. Photography has provided a voice to explore all that surrounds me and through its near instantaneous feedback, offered a means to express myself in a way that no other medium could.

Photo Ed Heffron

Busker

Artifacts

Lidderdale

Lincoln Highway

Colo

Bob Black

Publication of the Ice Cube Press Est. 1993

This particular book uses Minion type in various forms—regular, **bold**, **semi-bold**, *italics* & display as well as SMALL CAPITALS. When not using Minion, Adobe Garamond Pro has been used in a *variety* **of** *methods*.

Each Ice Cube Press book uses as much old & traditional letterpress & book design technique as we have learned at the time of publication, or as makes sense.

Ice Cube Press Printer Device Designed By Andrew Driscoll

testing hamburgeffonstiv
testing hamburgeffonstiv
123 *hamburgeffonstiv*
hamburgeffonstiv
hamburgeffonstiv
HAMBURGEFFONSTIV
"©&1234567890,."

Minion

testing hamburgeffonstiv
testing *hamburgeffonstiv*
123 **hamburgeffonstiv**
HAMBURGEFFONSTIV
"©&1234567890,."

Adobe Garamond Pro

Additional Harvest Books

▲ Voices of the Prairie: Three Poets of the Prairie. Featuring the work of Paul Engle, James Hearst and William Stafford. An exploration on how and why each of these "master" poets used the Midwest to find strength and soul for their writing. Also includes a foreword by Iowa poet **Michael Carey**. "Try these poets!…welcome to the farm."—*Wapsipincon Almanac*, $9.95

▲ Prairie Roots: Harvest Lecture 2001. This collection of Midwest themes includes an original essay by **Paul Gruchow** on naturalists Henry David Thoreau, John Muir, Rachel Carson and E.O. Wilson. Poetry by **Mary Swander**, essays by **Joni Kinsey** about prairie landscape painting, **Robert Sayre** on the formation and effects of the 'grid' system up on the land and **Thomas Dean** regarding the influence of migration. Also a small collection of photography by **Rev. Howard Vrankin**, $11.95

▲ The Tin Prayer: Words of the Wolverine. Written while artist-in-resident at the Island Institute in Sitka, Alaska this book is a confessionary tribute to growing up and making sense of the Midwest. "Part-memoir, part-manifesto, written with the naïve hutzpah of great folk art!"—*Little Village News*, $11.95

To order, send check & mailing address to:
Harvest Books—Ice Cube Press
205 N Front St. North Liberty, Ia. 52317
Shipping is free!
fmi: icecube@inav.net
or www.icecubepress.com